Catching Bats
Takes Patience

First published in 2015 by
Liberties Press
140 Terenure Road North | Terenure | Dublin 6W
T: +353 (1) 405 5701 | E: info@libertiespress.com | W: libertiespress.com

Trade enquiries to Gill & Macmillan Distribution
Hume Avenue | Park West | Dublin 12
T: +353 (1) 500 9534 | F: +353 (1) 500 9595 | E: sales@gillmacmillan.ie

Distributed in the United Kingdom by
Turnaround Publisher Services
Unit 3 | Olympia Trading Estate | Coburg Road | London N22 6TZ
T: +44 (0) 20 8829 3000 | E: orders@turnaround-uk.com

Distributed in the United States by
Casemate-IPM | 22841 Quicksilver Dr | Dulles, VA 20166
T: +1 (703) 661-1586 | F: +1 (703) 661-1547 | E: ipmmail@presswarehouse.com

ISBN: 978-1-909718-98-2
2 4 6 8 10 9 7 5 3 1

A CIP record for this title is available from the British Library.

Cover design by Karen Vaughan – Liberties Press
Internal design by Liberties Press

Catching Bats
Takes Patience

Mary Kennelly

Contents

For my mom and for my dad,
With love and gratitude.
—Moll

It's only words

Every day you think to show your love for me
By simply being here.
You do not understand, foolish one,
That woman feeds on fairytales
And loves the poet's silver tongue.

Just once I long to draw
Some aching words of desperate love.
Oh to be Cathy, cursed but adored
For all her faults and flaws.

Can't you understand that buried deep
Inside of me is still the little girl who thinks
'If I could force such passionate tirades,
I might still lose my soul to hell
And count myself well pleased'.

Tenderness

I think of you
In those first few moments
When I wake
And I smile
To know that you walk
Somewhere on this earth
Even though you are
No longer mine.

Inside the web

Child, let the world have what parts of you it will.
Our bond is far too deep for any others to take part,
A silken web of secret smiles and heartfelt hugs
And little laughs at jokes that only we can know.
We build our love on bedtime tales of all the day's events,
And making fairy cakes for tea parties when no else is home.
It is a loving that is understood and shared by us alone.

Moonlight waiting

When he woke I rushed to comfort him,
I kissed his tear-stained cheeks
And held his sobbing form,
I shushed and sang to him,
Promised that I would stay with him
To scare away whatever monsters came.
I rocked him back and forth until he slept –
A silver angel under heaven's glow.
I wonder if you're waiting under moonlight too:
Mother, awake, terrified,
Loving your child as I love mine.
Facing monsters you cannot hope to beat?
While oilmen, dressed in suits, tell me
That you and he are nothing more
Than acceptable collateral damage,
In their just and unavoidable war.

Death's tango

Hunger sends her out – the dance begins.
Slicing wind, she glides across the sky.
The smaller birds in desperation
Hurl themselves at her
To break her fearful rhythm.
But all to no avail – for now she stops,
Suspended in mid-air, eyes locked,
Until with deadly pirouette she dives,
Determined now as any lover, and seeks
Talons on flesh – Death's tango.

Amergin

And in the end who did you hurt, only you?
Throwing away loves like old clothes,
Tearing them one by one from your body
And casting them out to the cold.

And in the end who paid the price, only you?
Chasing obsession like breath,
Surrendering peace for the word,
Sacrificing all of the rest up to death.

And in the end who was bereft, only you?
Alone, as you walked through the rain
With a lifetime of love left behind you
As we, at a distance, despaired for your pain.

Raindrops keep falling

Born in the passion of a tempest,
Its rainbow beauty all on show
Against my windowpane.
Seeming, at first, strong enough
To carve its own path
Until descent began.
Slowly, silently, it spent itself.
No burst of sun to end its reign,
Just constant little loss.
There in that one innocent raindrop
I find the story of us.

Beyond compare

Oh no baby, you did not age well.
Whatever beauty once you had,
That passing gift of youth,
Has long since gone.
You wear the battles of a lifetime
On your lined and craggy face,
Like medals of honour
You embrace your sacrifices.
You are grey where you were once tan,
Soft where once you were strong,
Bald where you once had hair,
Have hair where there should be none.
Oh yes baby, I suppose it's just as well
That I'm running right beside you
In the ageing stakes.
My eyesight's fading anyway.
And I still love your touch and taste and smell.

Getting too big for my boots

In my uncle's pub, reading poetry again,
At four o'clock he wandered in
While I continued on.
When done, he asked if I was an American.
'Oh no,' I said, 'sure I'm from here.'
He was surprised, he said.
In jest, I told him I was shy,
As he drank down his beer.
'Don't be one bit shy to read them poems
In public, girl, they're not too bad at all,
And in truth you read them well enough
And your electrocution's good and all.'

Bicycle on a tightrope

Roll up, roll up! Come and see me try
To balance on a bicycle
A hundred feet up in the air.
Watch my desperate struggle
As I juggle fans and pedal
On a tightrope of despair.
You won't be alone, my friends,
In laughing right out loud,
As it takes all my might
Not to simply fall
And break upon the ground
Christ! I'm such a funny sight.
While an audience of
Watchful cats look on
And lick their lips with glee,
All that stands between them
And supper now,
In this circus world, is me.

Odyssey

Of course the intervening years
And adult eyes hold their own power
Over memory,
But they are not enough to
Deconstruct our childhood story.
We followed you as loyal acolytes
From my parents' kitchen
To your parents' pub as you mocked
The stern gods of our world and they smiled.
You were too dazzling for them to take offence.
You took that city and its exalted ones
By the throat – and they adored you for it.
We loved you too,
Our day darker when you said goodbye
At the door of your theatre of words and song.
You gave us all tenpence
To buy lemonade and sweets.
We would willingly have sacrificed our treats
 To stay with you, more enraptured
Than those children that had
Blithely followed the piper's tune.
We craved the magic of your mind –
To us you were Erato or Apollo
Or Eris – lover of sweet anarchy.

Worry

Crouching low, ready to swell,
It keeps me on my toes,
I am unsure, I am uncomfortable.

An iron train-track from my gut
Up into my mouth
That can't be moved, that can't be cut.

It creeps and crawls along my skin
And whispers as it goes,
'You cannot breathe, you cannot win.'

It speeds my heart, then sends it faster
'Til there can be no doubt
I am just a shivering slave, and it a savage master.

Wood turner

After the excitement, he is afraid.
What if he has not the skill
To free the soul he sees in me?
To him I am not over-coarse or common,
I am a miracle waiting only for his touch.
While he works he sits bent over,
Later on his back will pay,
But that does not matter now,
As, tongue between his teeth,
Beads of sweat begin to form,
And time and again his fingers find my grain,
Until I am set free, exposed.
Then he sets me down
And walks away.

Lament for a lost child

I weep every day for you, my lost child,
Now frozen in memory and time.
But I'm haunted far more by the things lost to you –
Your future lives only in mind.
No falling in love for the very first time,
No heartache when she turns away.
No debs ball, no study, no college,
No first job and blowing your pay
On things that I don't quite approve of.
No first flat with cups in the sink,
No arguments over your girlfriend,
No winning her back with a wink.
No tears to fall on your wedding,
No children of your own to hold,
No first house in need of repairs,
No slowing down, no growing old.
I grieve every day for the loss of you, child,
But it's your loss that drives my grief wild.

All that remains

On those seldom times I stop and think of you,
All that remains of all that we were
Is a small dull ache in my chest.
I have not forgotten the darker parts of us,
The sting of our love's failure,
But it no longer seems to matter –
The passing years have made it so.
I live instead the memories of sunny days,
The joy I found in knowing you.
She knows you better now as he knows me,
And I would not wish it any other way,
At least not any more.
You are a little piece of driftwood,
Whitened and washed up on my heart's shore.

Memoir

Scraped out across the page
Like butter on cold toast,
Old memories and hurts are trotted out,
Old tragedies, old ghosts.
You cast me out unto the wolves,
And taint my contribution.
You say this is a healing thing
But it tastes of retribution.

Sibling rivalry

All the evening,
Taken by the search
From plush hotels
To ever-stale,
Dark, early bars.
Down, down, down –
Or so it seemed.
Until at last
You found him,
Cranky and incoherent,
Hurling snatches of abuse.
You took his weight
Without a word
And led him home,
Made one quick
Bite of food,
Removed his shoes,
And left him
Snoring in his bed.
Years later and on the dry,
He still hasn't forgotten –
Or forgiven – you.

Lost for words?

When he talked of love,
He talked of old men
Parting young girls' thighs,
And of the cruel pranks
Played by feckless boys.
He talked of lusts
That might be slaked
And then just left behind.
He could be eloquent enough
About his love of land and sea,
Of heroic stories told
'Round dwindling fires
And the glory days
When he was young.
It took me years to realise
The deficit was in his heart
Not on his tongue.

Suffer little children

Sticky hands and
Hot stale breath.
Fumbling, groping, grunting.
While finest minds decide
What canon law allows.
Suffer little children.
Little children suffered.
Violated, buggered, raped.
Isolated, bribed, betrayed.
Which the greatest hurt?
And in the middle of it all,
Battered and bruised,
Christ lies bleeding still.

Choices

You choose unpleasant words
In front of all to set me down
And put me in my place

                        I choose laughter.

You choose to diminish
My triumphs and to cast
A cloud upon my joys

                        I choose laughter.

You choose whenever possible
To step out of your way
If it means you can block mine

                        I choose laughter.

You choose not to say
A single well-intentioned word
When pain fills up my heart

                    I choose laughter.

You go ahead and choose
Whatever little act you will.
You see it doesn't matter

                    I choose laughter.

I choose laughter
And joy
And all good things.

                    I choose laughter.

Love song

Heart-sore in a world where such a fate
Befalls two young girls in bright red shirts,
How will I now protect my trinity
From a force I do not understand?
Overwhelmed, I find no words
To alleviate my fears,
Until you sit in tender silence
And simply hold my hand.

Chivalry

When she said her husband was a gentle man,
That other woman made a joke and laughed:
'God help us missus, sure that won't do at all.
Between the sheets you want a man that's man enough
To know what he's about and strains with lust.'
'Oh, I don't know,' was her reply,
'I like my man to be chivalrous in the bedroom too –
With him it's always been a case of ladies first.'

Familiarity breeds . . .

I know the woman softly snoring in my bed.
There is nothing new in her,
No part of her I have not
Touched or seen before.
After twenty years with me
She is no longer young,
I know her greying hair and sagging breasts.
There are times when I would gladly
Stretch my hands across her throat
Just to have five minutes' peace.
I know that she would have me
Be more the poet
And whisper lies to her at night.
But what fine words would she have from me?
I am here, woman, because
There is nowhere else
That I would rather be.

Memory of a treasured manuscript
for John B.

Even after all this time
I cannot quite conceive
That you are truly gone.
Memories of a friendship shared
Still very much alive, as in
Some treasured manuscript.
And written there, in words
That no one else will ever use,
Lie all the gifts you shared –
Flashes of old roguery,
And the sting of old betrayals,
Loyalty, to stiffen the spine
Of one sometimes afraid,
Old stories, songs and poetry.
And laughter, always laughter –
A corner of your heart revealed
And living still in me.

Punishment

The music woke me up
To early morning winter dark.
I have been neglectful of my craft
These past few months.
Now this new dawn is filled
With unexpected promise.
Before long all those other things
I had set above the sound are gone.
I am the mad dog
Chasing the wild boar of song.
I only crave the tune.
But ill-use refuses to reward.
My words will not be moulded,
They jostle and jar and scorn the path
My meagre skill sets out.
Locked in this struggle,
I begin my day with failure,
The melody is gone.

Temper

In my anger the words pop and fizz
And collide inside my brain
Before they pour out,
Heedless of caution,
As a boiling, scarring shout.
I try for silence
But the sight of you
Is all it takes to spur them on.
I am light-headed with release,
Not caring yet about the reckoning
That will most surely come.

The medicine woman's lament

Is this what the carpenter would have wanted –
He, who knew so well the flight of birds
And the growing ways of the mustard tree,
Who caressed the grape and grain between his hands,
Who sang his thanks to the tender breeze
And allowed the gentle donkey to take him to his death
At the will of those who could not understand his ways?
If he could love the men, who in fear had run away,
Did he not love, all the more, the women who,
In spite of fear, made the choice to stay,
With herbs and salves to tend his needs as he slipped from
    the world?

Our kind has walked this earth since it began.
Listening to the growing pains of life,
Learning which plants would cool and which would burn,
Singing out the silent messages of birds and bees and animals,
Worshipping the hands that set the balance of all living things,
Attending to the births and deaths of generations,
Battling fever, sickness, wounds, with prayer and herbs,
Selling harmless potions to clear the skin and put
A sparkle in the eyes of lovelorn girls in quest of men.

Ignorance of our ways meant we were feared as well as loved,
But we were always known as wise, until
You named us witch and claimed our knowledge came from dark,
And that we must burn before our poison spread,
Because we would not honour father without mother –
Though even a child knows this cannot be –
And because we would not go on bended knee
To men who hate all female kind.
And yet before our ashes cooled, you sought to steal our ways
Bell, book, incense, golden chalice, robes and candle –
When did the carpenter ask for these?

January garden

After fruiting time the massacre began.
All the summer's mighty warriors,
Sprung from seed to feed and entertain,
Dug up and sent to rot.
Showy roses, cut back to size – bloom-time's over.
Flowerbeds, providers of a summer's pleasure
Hacked back, 'til black earth lies exposed.
The trees, the garden's supermodels,
Mere skeletons, all secrets now on show.
Life sacrificed to winter's grey.
Yet even after such a desecration,
Resurrection finds its way.

Regrets

Age played cruel tricks on him,
Bending over his bones until
He was never really free of pain.
It dimmed all sight and sound,
Leaving him in a world alone,
To rest with his regrets.
The fears of his childhood,
Fed by his mother, the priest
And even his friends,
As they swapped made-up secrets
On the ways of the world,
Seemed small now, and distant.
Finally he came to understand
That a life without pleasure
Was too high a price
For salvation of soul.
And those young girls
Who had once terrified him,
He remembered then as beautiful.
Brown limbs, wild hair and sweet smells
Invaded his dreams, tormenting him,
Beguiling him, so that winter and summer,
As he slowly, painfully pedalled
The one and a half miles to daily mass,

One thought captured him
And would not let him rest –
He even told his neighbour once –
If he ever got as far as godless London,
He'd invest right heavy
In one of them loose women,
And finally he could learn all about
The pleasures of the skin.

Mother's reward

Every day is soon filled up
With a thousand thankless tasks,
Most of which, it seems,
I must repeatedly repeat.
I wash, I iron, I fold,
I chop, I cook, I clean,
I scold the constant bickering,
I kiss the bloody knee,
And of course I take requests.
'Mummy, can my friend come
To our house today?'
'Can you teach me how to bake 'cause
Katie's mother has?'
'Mummy, can you find my football boots –
The match is on at half-past three?'
'Can we stop for Jamie
While we're on the way?'
'Mummy, can I have a drink?'
'Mummy, can we watch TV?'
'What time is dinner?'
'I need new shoes.'
'Oh Mum! You never take us anywhere.'
But finally, around about the time
I start to think that old shoe lady

Got it right, my golden moment comes.
They are all asleep, and I rejoice!
Blessed peace seeps slowly in,
Disturbed only by the faint thunder
Of the electric kettle.
It lasts for as long as a cup of tea,
After which the preparations for tomorrow
Must begin again.

Chrysalis

It was the smell that took me back
And I watched again from her bed
As, sitting at her dressing table,
She laid out all that she would need,
Serious as any surgeon at his craft.
Time for transformation to begin.
She gave the task her all:
Layer after layer she joined the dots
And coloured carefully between the lines;
A butterfly began to breathe,
Until, always at the last,
She coloured in her lips,
Then pursed to seal the colour fast.
My ordinary mother gone,
A fairy queen would turn
And smile and kiss me on the cheek.
But she did not hold me long
For he always came, arms out,
His eyes full of his pride in her.
He took her from us,
Leaving only memory,
Impossible to hold,
Growing ever fainter,
Like her lingering perfume.

Preparation for goodbye?

I watch as every day you grow one further step
Beyond the nest that, out of love, we made for you.
You cannot hide how much you seek the freedom
To feel warm air beneath your own as-yet-untested wings.
No longer really happy with all the things that I
Would bring and lay down at your feet, I must accept
My world grows small and ties you in.
When I think of all the struggles we have faced,
How could I have ever known that letting go
Would prove the most challenging?

Prince charming

In fairness, it's nothing like it promised in the story book.
Maybe we should sue that blasted fairy tale 'cause
To be honest our little castle soon got rather cramped
When you moved in all your rugby gear and magazines.
And three kids really do make a lot of mess and noise
As they hoover up our money, space and time,
And precious little else.
They also did for our spontaneous encounters
Upon the kitchen table.
Our passion – if you could call it that –
Now calls for military precision, five minutes on a Thursday night.
Inside I know I've betrayed the sisterhood but
I find it hard to be a feminist while picking
Smelly clothes up from the bedroom floors
And cooking endlessly same, stale dinners.
Even if you brought me champagne every day –
Which of course you don't –
Kids' homework with a hangover is the biggest pain on earth
And my liver just can't take it any more.
But still it has its compensations and I know
That you will be with me through all our mess
To reap the whirlwind of the life that we have sown
And you'll still come running with the loo roll
When it runs out while I'm sitting on my throne.

An overnight success

So many had their doubts,
In fact I did myself,
But here I am,
As I always believed
That I would be.
I finally got rich quick
On my seven-thousandth try
At the tender age of fifty-three.

Mommy talk

When my mommy says 'maybe',
What she really means is 'no'.
'No' is what she really means
For 'perhaps' and 'later on' also.
But if you can figure mommy,
Go ahead and be my guest,
'Cause when my mommy tells me 'no',
 Sometimes she means 'yes'.

Freedom of choice

It's always the ones I hardly know
That take my arm
And whisper in soft tones
About exhausting all our options
And the cross we have to bear.
They advise me not to worry,
That stress alone can be the cause.
The doctors can do anything these days.
Isn't it hard for a man, all the same –
Not having a son –
But there are children, crying out for love,
In China or Romania or Peru.

Why should I feel guilty or explain
To busybodies who hardly know my name,
That some of us are happy
To make different choices?

Treasure trove

When she is gone
They'll sort out all her stuff –
Clothes and shoes to charity
In seemingly endless bags –
Jewellery, paintings, ornaments –
All divided out or sold –
The books, to God knows where.
Then they'll find the box,
Her lifelong treasure chest.
Inside, a silver-plated wedding coin,
First locks, first shoes, first teeth,
A plastic holy-water bottle,
Price intact at thirty pence,
Gift from a three-year-old,
Home-made birthday cards,
Baptismal candles, a christening gown,
Her list with weights and times and dates,
Copies, pictures, drawings.
Cardboard-encased memory.

The road home

When she first went with him,
Exile sat lightly on her skin.
It was enough for her to pay
A duty call home once a week.
Later when her own clan grew old,
She took her brood with a heavy heart
Along that road each and every day,
Her life bound up by duty and decay,
Until only ghosts remained
To call her, more and more,
Through the passing years,
To go to their graves
In remembrance, to kneel and pray.
Yet after almost forty years,
Grandchildren yapping at her feet,
She did not buy the painting
That showed her house or street,
She took no time for second thought.
The painting of the road to home
Is the painting that she bought.

Back to earth

Of course my mother's heart
Swelled with pride
When my little girl said
She wanted to grow up
To be like me.
That she would write books
Just like mine,
Full of all kinds of poetry –
Except hers would rhyme!

That letter

Perhaps it would have been better after all,
If I had sent you the letter that I wrote
The day after we argued.

You might have read it –
And understood the reasons for
My anger and my hurt.

And it might have been enough
For me to know you knew
What you had damaged with your words.

But, coward that I am, I told myself
The writing not the reading was the thing
That mattered in the end.

And so we remained –
Shattered.

Grief

I am jealous of the tired-looking woman
In the baggy tracksuit on the 46A bus.
She has him to share her shopping with,
While there is nothing left of us.

I am angry with my friend when she complains
Of her husband's mess and all that she must do.
I wish I had not let such unimportant things
Fill up my too-short a time with you.

A hard winter

This is a hard winter.
For weeks now, subdued green
Has struggled to peek out
From underneath a duvet
Of sparkling white.
The horses and cows are all in –
Even the last few late stragglers
Who had frost, set as hard
As the ground, on their backs.
Plover and snipe
Come to visit our once-boggy fields
Where frozen hoof marks
Make for easier pecking.
They pay their way, rewarding
Us with sky-filled ballets,
Playing follow-my-leader
Through clear pale blue skies.
Closer again, tits and finches,
Having stripped the holly and cotoneaster
Absolutely bare,
Eat in worried watchful snatches
From the bird table
Outside my kitchen window.
We change their water dishes

Twice each day –
My boys enamoured
Of the icy water-pucks they get
As profit for the task.
Our dogs lie huddled
Inside a bower of pampas grass,
Keeping a close eye on the door –
And their chance at the fire.
We have our worries too:
Are the water pipes still running?
Is there always enough fuel?
How do we brave skating-rink roads
On our way to visit older neighbours
Or shops or school or work?

Unintended monument

Dead televisions –
Plastic and glass piled high –
A funeral pyre
Beside Limerick's Dock Road.
No more stories left
For them to tell or learn.
The centre of the house
For countless hours and lives
Become just so much waste.
Who saved, who stole, who coveted,
Of no importance now.

Words and music and song

Did we have enough things,
Do you think?
Small electrical devices that
Dated as we took them from the box
And waterproof flat-screen plasma TVs
Did we really need them,
Do you think?
Our one-bedroom furnished
Apartments in Bulgaria
And sporty new-reg SUVs.
Was it worth it,
Do you think?
Our glory daze, our swagger,
Champagne, cocaine parties
And all our get-rich ways?
What will we tell them,
Do you think?
When they wait to see the doctor
And sit in overcrowded classrooms
Without their SNAs?
Will they be forgiving,
Do you think?

When they just can't find a job
And sing at parties through their tears
 'Last one out may close the door'.
And are we broken,
Do you think?
Are all of our tomorrows worthless –
Thrown away with last year's junk.
Were we never something more?

Dinner for Siobhan Reidy's fortieth birthday

Siobhan Reidy is late on the night,
But we see no harm in that,
It took us a misfiring month
To get our calendars to coincide.
We bought her a painting,
The one about wanting to be free.
We talk about the days when
We were magnificent at seventeen,
The boys we loved with all our hearts,
The many frogs we'd kissed.
Maureen Kennelly made me laugh
So much I nearly peed –
That's what three pregnancies will do to you.
Siobhan Reidy – the wild child –
Played mother to Siobhan Sweeney's plans
For dealing with our teenagers and sex.
We ate good food, drank three bottles of wine,
Flirted with the waiter, who flirted back,
Earning gratitude – and a big tip.
We laughed and laughed and laughed.

We didn't mention even once
The dimming of our hearts,
Loves broken and betrayed,
Crosses carried mile by mile,
A beautiful son lost.
The four of us older, struggling,
But trying to stand tall.
Isn't that worth something?
Maybe we are magnificent after all.

Dressing up

He thinks I waxed my lip
And chin and legs for him
And plucked my brows
And washed my hair
And trowelled this make-up on.

He admired my dress
Which cost so much –
He'd shake if he but knew.
He didn't even notice
My dizzyingly high, high-heeled shoes.

He doesn't have a clue
About my need to have
The very latest, current-season bag
And yet more bling, bling, bling,
But you do, sister – you do.

Dear deceptively simple

Although it's liked by simple folk,
Your poetry does not fit our needs.
Where lies the gain for us in teaching
Your deceptively simple lines,
Your no-false-rails, your country rhymes?
There are no sharp conundrums
Or technical dexterities that we
Might torture students with unpicking
To show our clever brains.
Although you're eloquent, you're easy.
You have no sound for sound or form for form.
And while it might well be subversive,
Your poetry has only truth –
And what is there to learn from that?

English class

Do I still love them
As I loved them once,
When they were new
And stirred my teenage heart,
Now that I have held them
For a score of years
And forced them to trot before
Students who do not care
And look at me with dull eyes
As I take apart each
Image and emotion they contain?

No – I do not love them
In that desperate way any more.
They are grown tame;
Their mystery is gone.
They are as unexceptional
As any other group
Of verbs and nouns
That one might casually construct,
Part only of a course
That must be covered,
If possible, before the Mocks.

And yet sometimes,
On a very seldom day,
When I think it can no longer happen still,
One of them will
Catch me out again,
Refusing to be mundane,
Insisting I recognise its power.
Then I must find my breath
And fight back tears
As I read it to my class.

February tests

The first exam begins.
Silent girls in once-neat rows
Create a constant rustle,
Tapping, coughing, shuffling, dropping.
Soon all heads are bowed except
Those few that scan the room for inspiration.
They know the rules,
Avoid the supervisor's eye.
In a blink, only one hour left.
The ticking hand of the exam-room clock
Fills any lulling moment.
Those that are too soon run out
Of things to say sit nervously
As others from their class still write away.
Just how long is a piece of string?
And time runs on and on and on
Until the last 'Pens down'.

Dust up

Wife and mother gone,
The woman you came home to was a hag,
Saggy sweatpants, greasy hair and deadly eyes.
She hadn't time, all day, to make the dinner –
Not that you remember asking her to –
Sausages and chips will have to do,
She says, daring you to disagree.
She's been on a cleaning spree again,
Black bags stuffed full with papers,
Magazines, out-of-date food and old clothes –
Probably yours – litter every room,
Asylum-seekers doomed to face the backyard bonfire
As she mercilessly destroys the things
That, not so long ago, she just had to have.
And her angry stance is screaming that it's all your fault,
You, who never bought a bloody scented candle in your life!
Well, you've nothing to do but ride out the storm,
Until that hellion is gone and in her trail,
Punch-drunk and vaguely repentant,
Returning slowly, comes your wife.

Retribution

Something snapped and broke free
And grew inside of him.
It tingled and bubbled and boiled
Up from his fingers and toes,
Beyond his power to control.
It screamed for retribution,
For a million past wrongs,
As it licked along his spine.
He looked at the smugly smiling
Face of his brother,
His tormentor,
Three years older,
Three years stronger,
Three years faster,
And he knew, he knew,
That if he hit him,
It might well be
The last thing that he would ever do.
His brother would kill him,
He knew, he knew.
He landed one almighty blow
And, turning on his heels, he flew.

While I am away

While I am away – I miss you.
I miss those almost imperceptible changes
That sweep you, day by day, to adulthood.
I miss the first times or last times
For words or songs or turns of phrase;
I miss those dances that can never be regained.
I miss your sunshine and your showers,
Your tantrums and your tears.
I miss the moment after moment after moment
That grows silently into lost years.
I am greedy for the parts of you I miss –
While I am away.

Casual contact

Introduced by a casual acquaintance,
We met. I smiled and shook your hand.
Then we moved on with our day.
Until, a little later on,
Alerted by some near-forgotten sense,
I turned and found you watching me.
Embarrassed to be caught,
You quickly dropped your eyes and blushed,
As though a score of intervening years
Had somehow slipped away and, once again,
You stood between a boy and man,
Caught doing something you should not.
You didn't realise, that in your travelling back
You had also carried me.
I was once again that girl
Who loved to laugh and flirt,
Untempered yet by responsibility.

The court fool

Jester, sing for your supper.
Charm and entertain us
And we'll tell you
We love you
And your work,
Even though we talked
While you sang.

A poem for Colm

'Don't look behind,' you said, Mummy,
Don't look behind as I jumped
Or soared through the air for the sliothar.
'Don't look behind,' you said, Mum.

'Don't look behind,' you said, Mummy,
I was yours for too short of a span
But I'm travelling the road still beside you.
'Don't look behind,' you said, Mum.

'Don't look behind,' you said, Mummy,
Though you cherished each one of my smiles
And my tears and my laughter and tantrums.
'Don't look behind,' you said, Mum.

'Don't look behind,' you said, Mummy,
And I didn't – or tried not to do
I'm reaching for dreams in the stars now
And I won't look behind me now, Mum.